EASY PIANO

MY FIRST
ROCK
SONG BOOK
A TREASURY OF HITS THROUGH THE DECADES

ISBN 978-1-4950-6290-2

HAL•LEONARD®
7777 W. BLUEMOUND RD. P.O. BOX 13819 MILWAUKEE, WI 53213

T0066170

Visit Hal Leonard Online at
www.halleonard.com

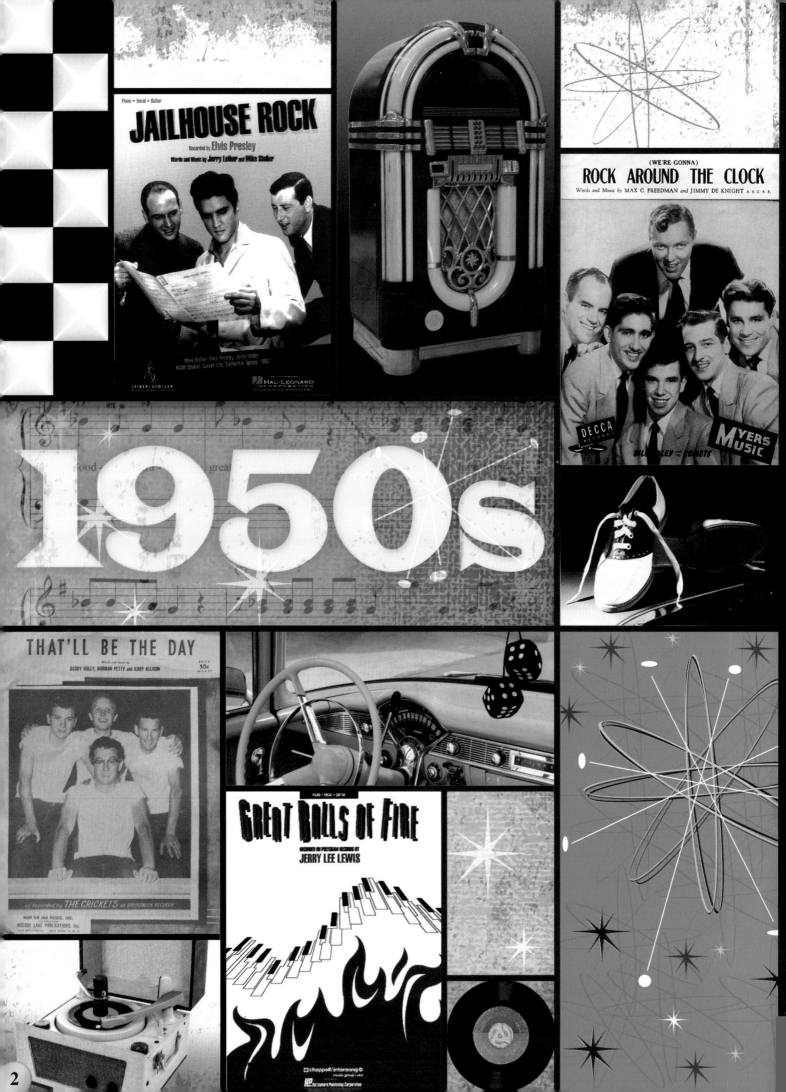

GREAT BALLS OF FIRE

Words and Music by JACK HAMMER
and OTIS BLACKWELL

With a solid Rock beat

You shake my nerves and you rat - tle my brain. __

Too much love drives a man in - sane. __ You broke my will,

but what a thrill. Good - ness, gra - cious, great balls of fire!

I laughed at love 'cause I thought it was fun - ny. You came a - long and you

so kind, ___ I'm gon-na tell the world that you're mine, mine, mine, mine. ___

I chew my nails and I twid-dle my thumb. ___ I'm real ner-vous, but it

sure is fun. ___ Come on, ba - by, you're driv-ing me cra-zy.

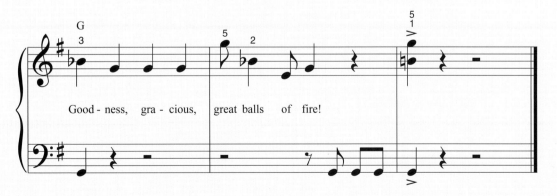

Good - ness, gra - cious, great balls of fire!

JAILHOUSE ROCK

Words and Music by JERRY LEIBER
and MIKE STOLLER

Moderate Rock

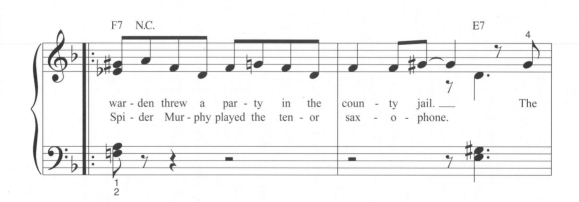

war - den threw a par - ty in the coun - ty jail. ___ The
Spi - der Mur - phy played the ten - or sax - o - phone.

prison band was there and they began to wail. ___ The

Little Joe was blowin' on the slide trombone. ___ The

band was jumpin' and the joint began to swing. ___ You

drummer boy from Illinois went crash, boom, bang. ___ The

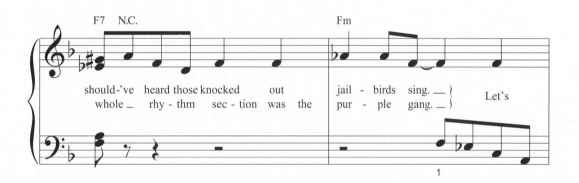

should-'ve heard those knocked out jailbirds sing. ___ } Let's

whole ___ rhythm section was the purple gang. ___ }

rock! Let's

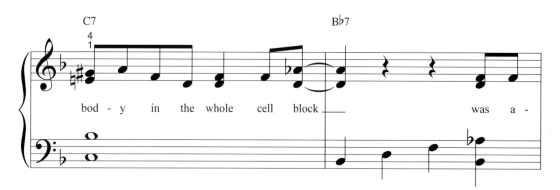

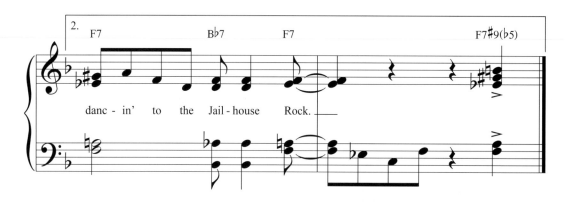

That'll Be the Day

Words and Music by JERRY ALLISON,
NORMAN PETTY and BUDDY HOLLY

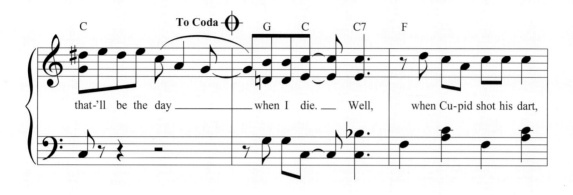

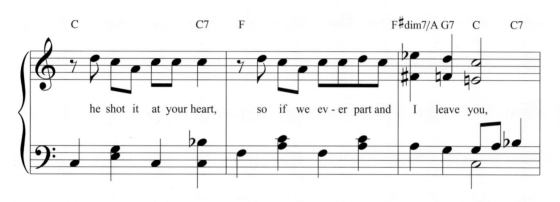

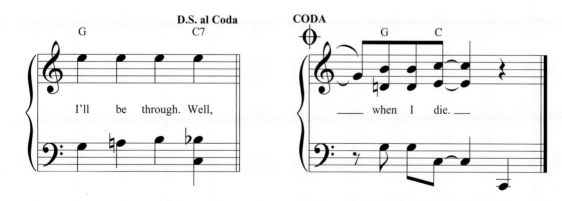

Rock Around the Clock

Words and Music by MAX C. FREEDMAN
and JIMMY DeKNIGHT

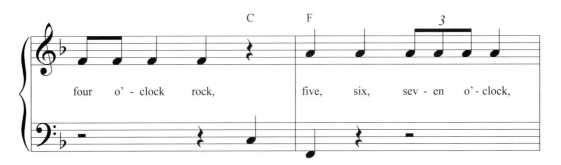

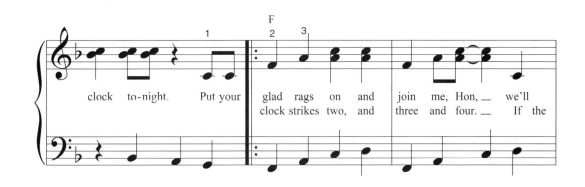

clock to-night. Put your glad rags on and join me, Hon, __ we'll
clock strikes two, and three and four. __ If the

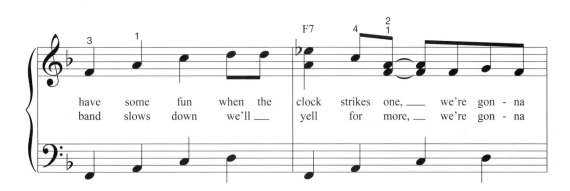

have some fun when the clock strikes one, __ we're gon - na
band slows down we'll __ yell for more, __ we're gon - na

rock a - round the clock to - night, __ we're gon - na
rock a - round the clock to - night, __ we're gon - na

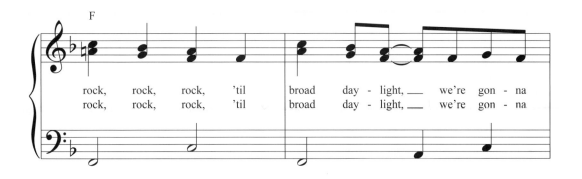

rock, rock, rock, 'til broad day - light, __ we're gon - na
rock, rock, rock, 'til broad day - light, __ we're gon - na

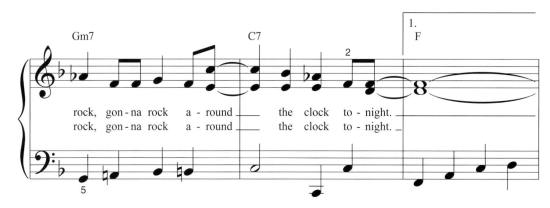

rock, gon-na rock a - round ___ the clock to - night.
rock, gon-na rock a - round ___ the clock to - night.

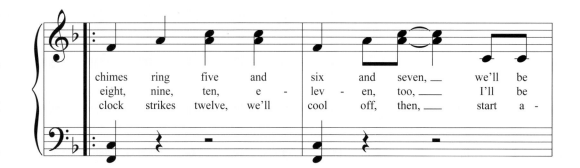

___ When the

When the

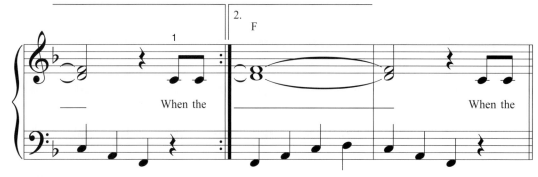

chimes ring five and six and seven, ___ we'll be
eight, nine, ten, e - lev - en, too, ___ I'll be
clock strikes twelve, we'll cool off, then, ___ start a -

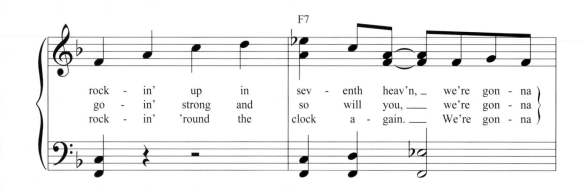

rock - in' up in sev - enth heav'n, ___ we're gon - na
go - in' strong and so will you, ___ we're gon - na
rock - in' 'round the clock a - gain. ___ We're gon - na

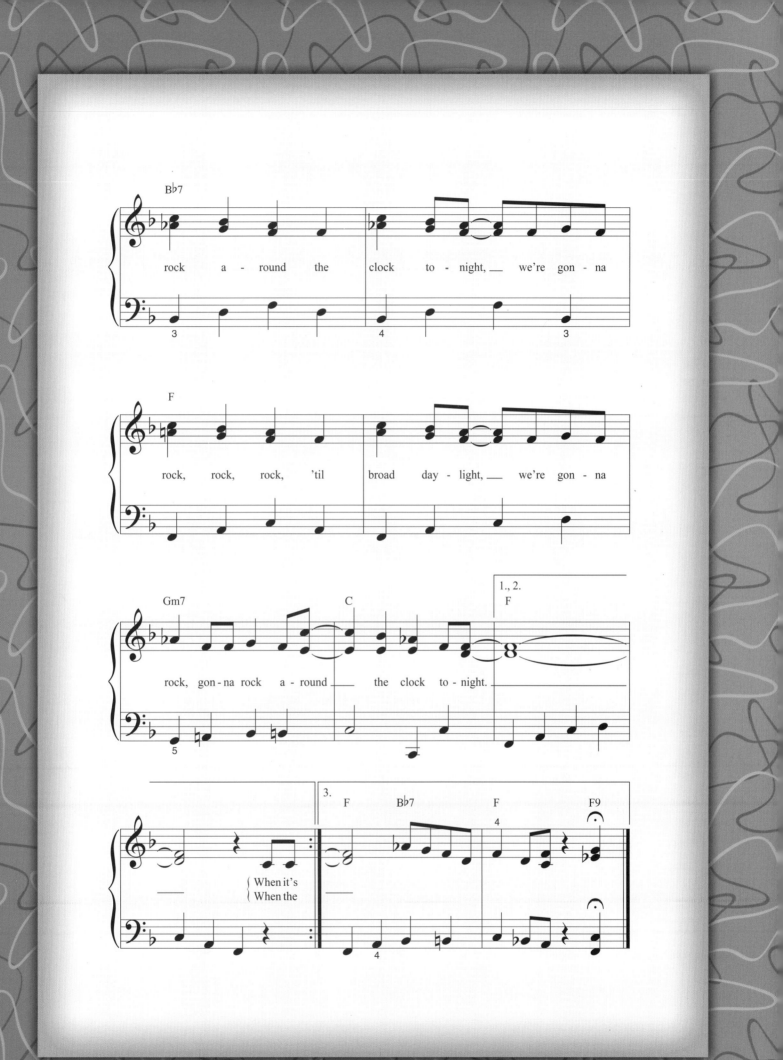

I WANT TO HOLD YOUR HAND

Words and Music by JOHN LENNON
and PAUL McCARTNEY

With a steady Rock beat

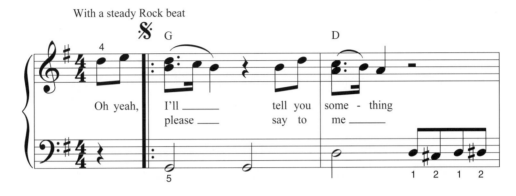

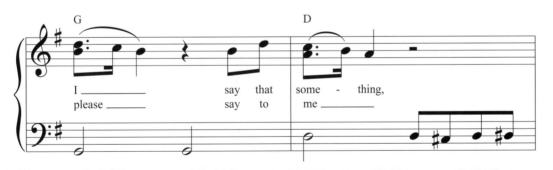

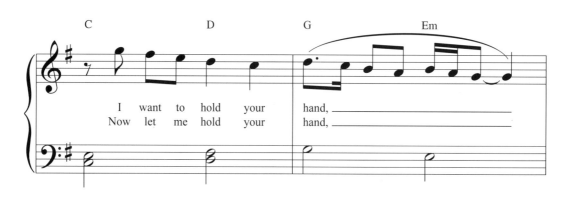

I want to hold your hand, _____
Now let me hold your hand, _____

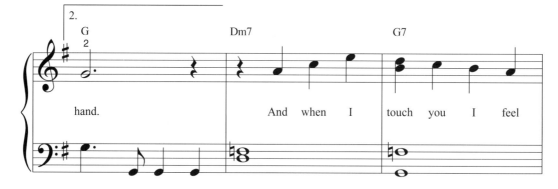

I want to hold your hand.   Oh, ____
I want to hold your

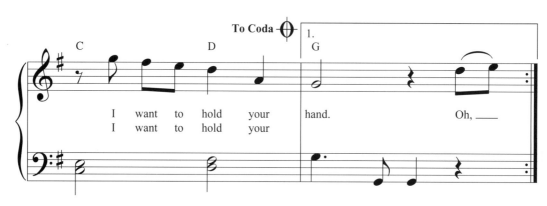

hand.   And when I touch you I feel

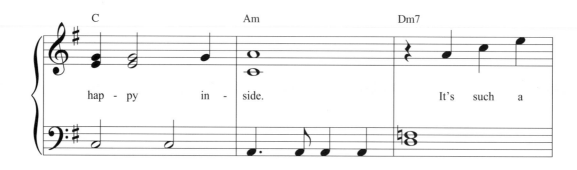

hap - py in - side.   It's such a

feel - ing that my love I can't hide, ___ I can't hide, __

D.S. al Coda
(verse 1)

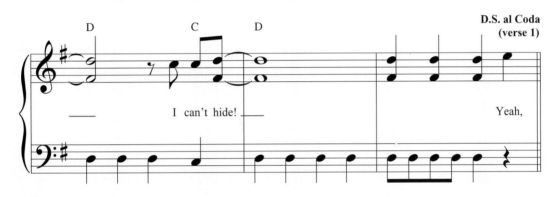

__ I can't hide! __ Yeah,

CODA

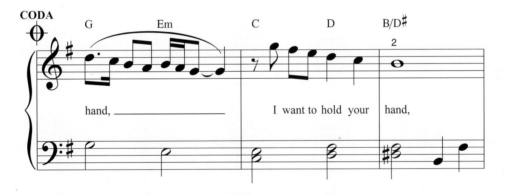

hand, ____ I want to hold your hand,

I want to hold your hand.

The Loco-Motion

Words and Music by GERRY GOFFIN
and CAROLE KING

Moderately fast

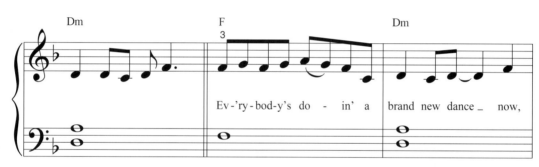

Ev-'ry-bod-y's do - in' a brand new dance _ now,

(Come on, ba-by, do ____ the lo-co-mo- tion.) I know you'll get to like it if you

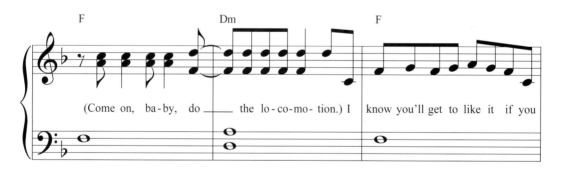

give it a chance _ now. (Come on, ba-by, do ____ the lo-co-mo- tion.) My

lit-tle ba-by sis - ter can do it with ease, __ it's eas-i-er than learn-in' your

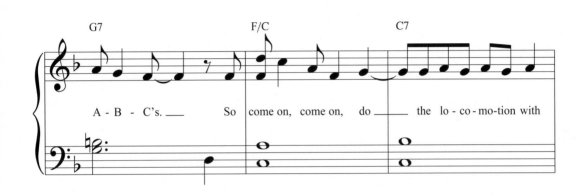

A - B - C's. __ So come on, come on, do __ the lo-co-mo-tion with

me. You got-ta swing your hips now. Come on,

ba-by, jump up, __ jump back. __ Oh, well, I

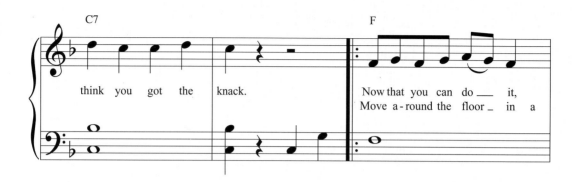

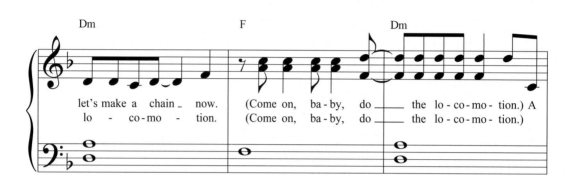

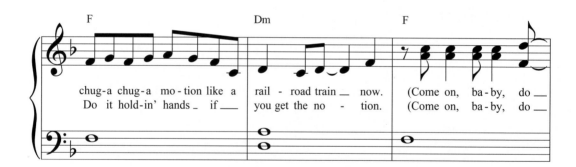

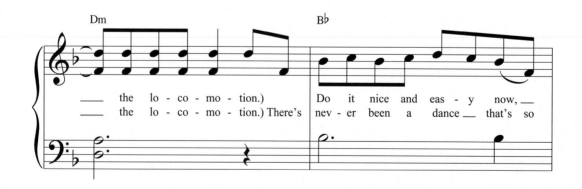

No Particular Place to Go

Words and Music by
CHUCK BERRY

With a Beat

Rid-ing a-long in my au-to-mo-bile,
bile,
go,
boose,

my ba-by be-side me at the wheel,
I was an-xious to tell her the way I feel.
so we parked way out on the co-ca-mo.
still try-ing to get her belt un-loose.

I stole a kiss at the turn of a mile,
So I told her soft-ly and sin-cere,
The night was young and the moon was gold,
All the way home I held a grudge,

my cu-ri-os-i-ty run-ning
and she leaned and whis-pered in my
so we both de-cid-ed to take a
for the safe-ty belt that would-n't

wild.
ear.
stroll.
budge.

Cruis-ing and play-ing the ra - di -
Cud - dling more — and driv - ing
Can you i - mag-ine the way I
Cruis-ing and play-ing the ra - di -

o,
slow,
felt?
o,

with no par - tic - u - lar place to
with no par - tic - u - lar place to
I could-n't un - fas - ten her safe - ty
with no par - tic - u - lar place to

1.–3.
F   N.C.

go.
go.
belt.

Rid - ing a - long in my au - to - mo -
No — par - tic - u - lar place — to
Rid - ing a - long in my cal - a -

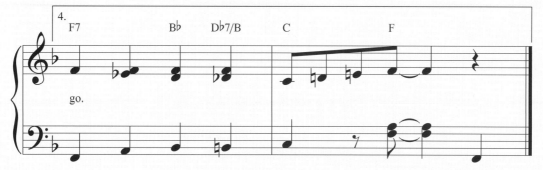

4.
F7   Bb   Db7/B   C   F

go.

Words and Music by
CHUCK BERRY

You'd see them wear - ing their bag - gies, ____
We'll all be gone for the sum - mer ____

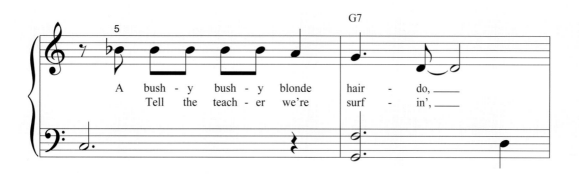

huar - a - chi san - dals, too. ____
we're on sa - far - i to stay. ____

A bush - y bush - y blonde hair - do, ____
Tell the teach - er we're surf - in', ____

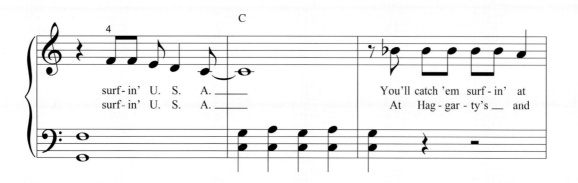

surf - in' U. S. A. ____
surf - in' U. S. A. ____

You'll catch 'em surf - in' at
At Hag - gar - ty's ___ and

Del Mar, ___ Ven - tu - ra Coun - ty Line, _
Swam - i's ___ Pac - if - ic Pal - i - sades,

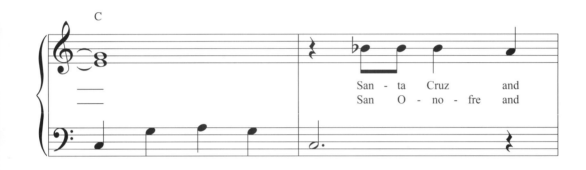

___ San - ta Cruz and
___ San O - no - fre and

Tress - els, ___ Aus - tra - lia's Nar - a - bine. _
Sun - set, ___ Re - don - do Beach, L. A. ___

___ All o - ver Man -
___ All o - ver La

hat - tan _____ and down Do - he - ny way. _
Jol - la, _____ at Wai - a - me - a Bay. _

_____ Ev - 'ry - bod - y's gone
Ev - 'ry - bod - y's gone

surf - in', _____ surf - in' U. S. A. _
surf - in', _____ surf - in' U. S. A. _

1.
C

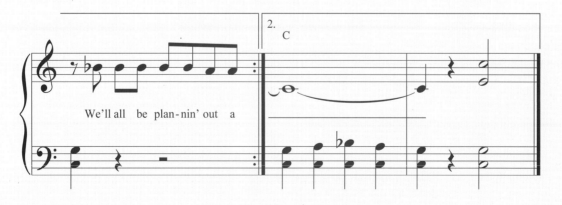

We'll all be plan - nin' out a

2.
C

Bohemian Rhapsody

Words and Music by
FREDDIE MERCURY

Slowly, freely

Is this the real life? Is this just fan-ta-sy?

Caught in a land-slide, no es-cape from re-al-i-ty.

O-pen your eyes, look up to the skies and see,

I'm just a poor boy, I need no sym-pa-thy be-cause I'm

easy come, easy go, little high, little low,

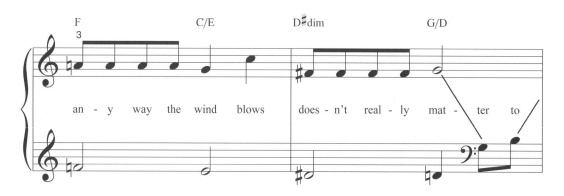

an - y way the wind blows does-n't real - ly mat - ter to

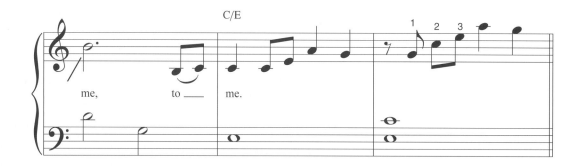

me, to ____ me.

Slowly, steady tempo

Ma - ma _____ just killed a man, put a
Too late, _____ my time has come, sends ____

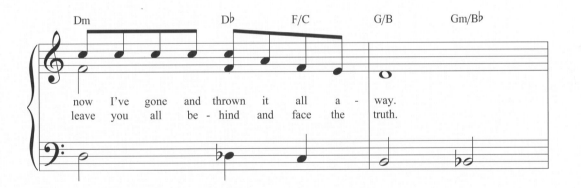

I'm not back a - gain this time to mor - row, car - ry on, car - ry
some-times wish I'd never been born at

on as if noth-ing real - ly mat - ters.

all.

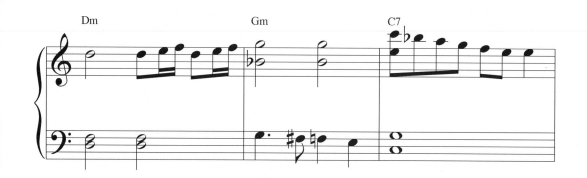

Double Time (♪ = ♩)

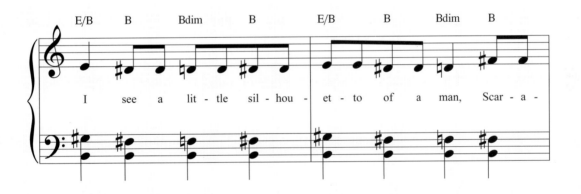

I see a lit - tle sil - hou - et - to of a man, Scar - a -

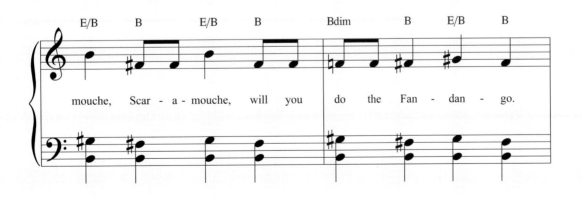

mouche, Scar - a - mouche, will you do the Fan - dan - go.

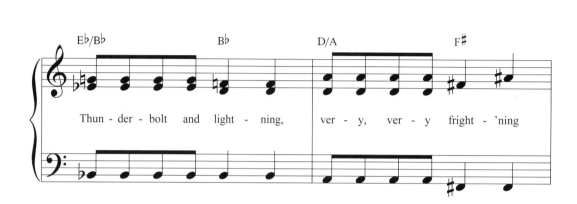

Thun - der - bolt and light - ning, ver - y, ver - y fright - 'ning

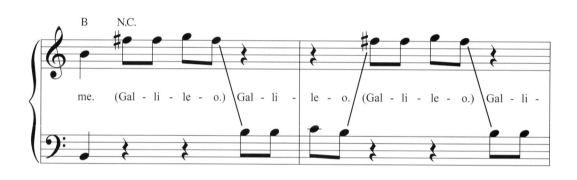

me. (Gal - li - le - o.) Gal - li - le - o. (Gal - li - le - o.) Gal - li -

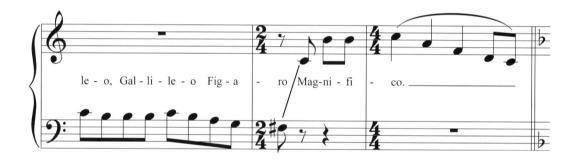

le - o, Gal - li - le - o Fig - a - ro Mag - ni - fi - co. _____

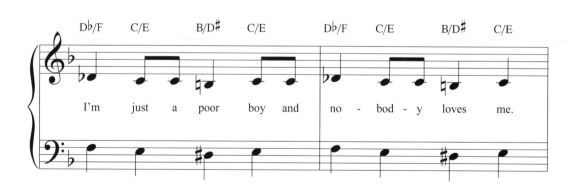

I'm just a poor boy and no - bod - y loves me.

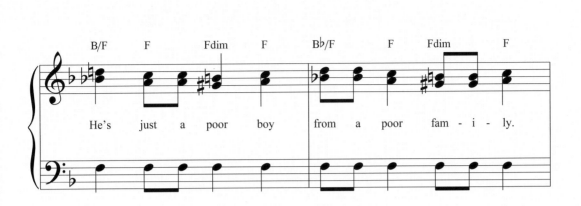

He's just a poor boy from a poor fam - i - ly.

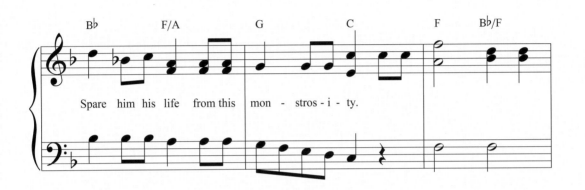

Spare him his life from this mon - stros - i - ty.

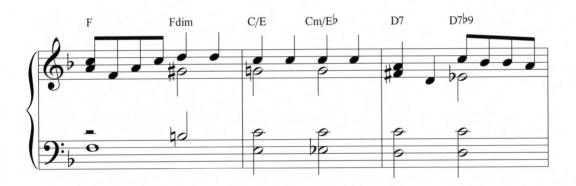

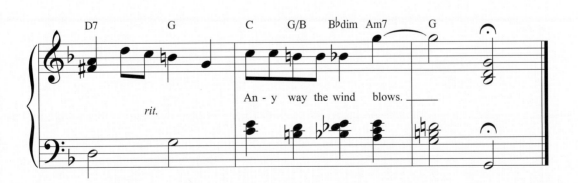

An - y way the wind blows.

Let It Be

Words and Music by JOHN LENNON
and PAUL McCARTNEY

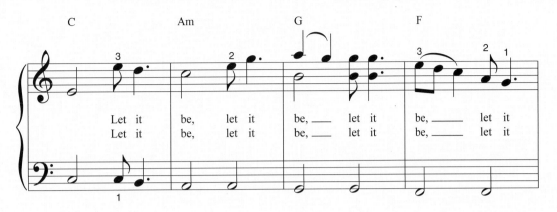

Let it be, let it be, _____ let it be, _____ let it
Let it be, let it be, _____ let it be, _____ let it

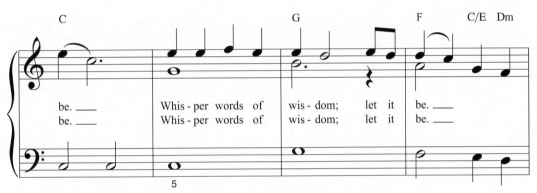

be. _____ Whis-per words of wis-dom; let it be. _____
be. _____ Whis-per words of wis-dom; let it be. _____

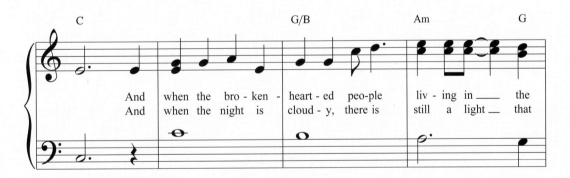

And when the bro-ken - heart-ed peo-ple liv-ing in _____ the
And when the night is cloud-y, there is still a light _____ that

world a - gree, there will be an an - swer; let it be. _____
shines on me. Shine un - til to - mor-row; let it be. _____

For | though they may be | part - ed, there is
I | wake up to the | sound of mu - sic,

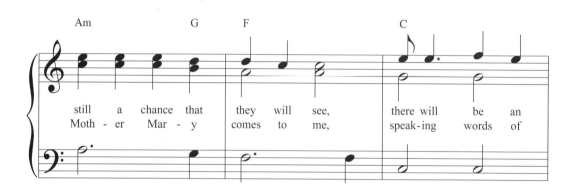

still a chance that | they will see, | there will be an
Moth - er Mar - y | comes to me, | speak-ing words of

an - swer; let it | be. ___ | | Let it be, let it
wis - dom; let it | be. ___ | | Let it be, let it

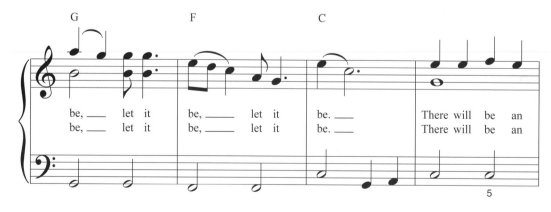

be, ___ let it | be, ___ let it | be. ___ | There will be an
be, ___ let it | be, ___ let it | be. ___ | There will be an

an - swer;   let it be. ____   Let it be,   let it
an - swer;   let it be. ____   Let it be,   let it

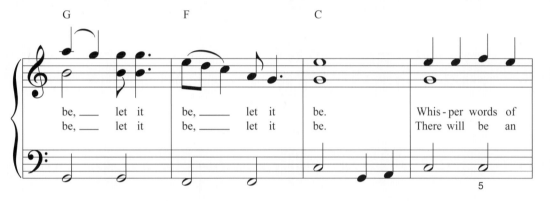

be, ____ let it   be, ____ let it   be.   Whis - per words of
be, ____ let it   be, ____ let it   be.   There will be an

wis - dom;   let it be. ____
an - swer;   let it be. ____   *(like a hymn)*

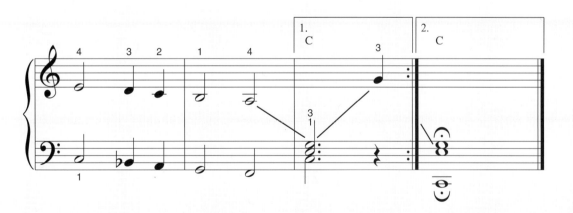

Crocodile Rock

Words and Music by ELTON JOHN
and BERNIE TAUPIN

Hard Rock, in 4

I re-mem-ber when rock was young, _____ me and

Su-sie had so much fun, _____ hold-ing hands and skim-min'

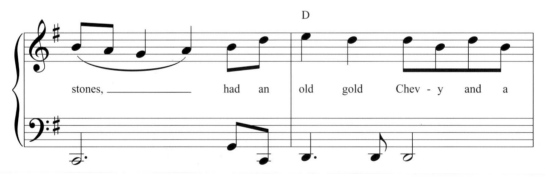

stones, _____ had an old gold Chev-y and a

place of my own. But the big-gest kick I ev-er

got _____ was doin' a thing called the Croc - o - dile

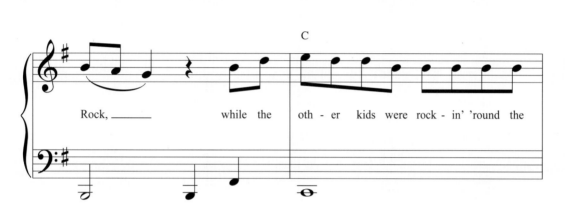

Rock, _____ while the oth - er kids were rock - in' 'round the

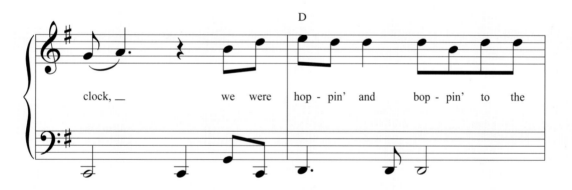

clock, __ we were hop - pin' and bop - pin' to the

Croc - o - dile Rock. Well, Croc - o - dile Rock - in' is

some-thing shock-in' when your feet just can't keep still. __

I nev-er knew me a bet-ter time and I guess I nev-er __

will. Oh, __ Law-dy, ma-ma, those Fri-day nights when

Su-sie wore __ her dress-es tight __ and the Croc-o-dile __ rock-in'

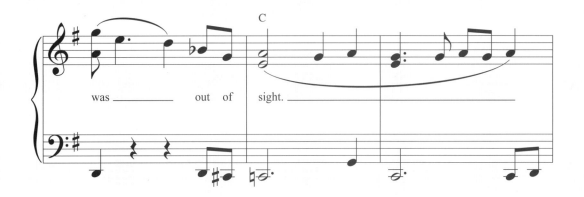

was _____ out of sight. _____

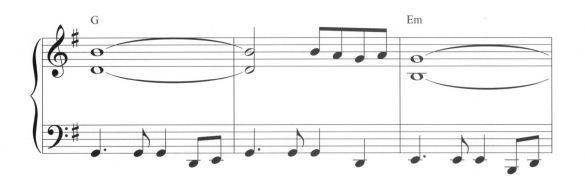

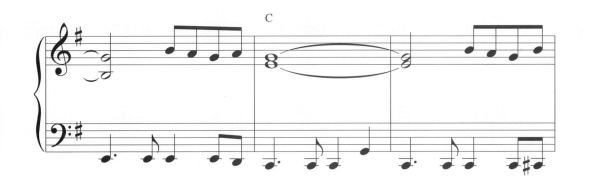

DANCING QUEEN

Words and Music by BENNY ANDERSSON,
BJÖRN ULVAEUS and STIG ANDERSON

Disco Rock

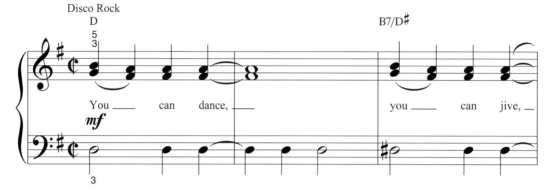

You ___ can dance, ___ you ___ can jive, ___

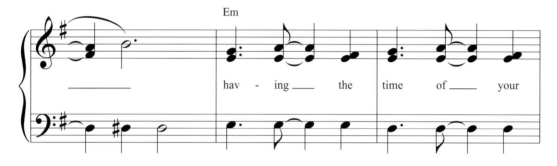

___ hav - ing ___ the time of ___ your

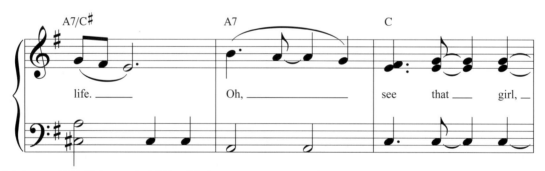

life. ___ Oh, _____ see that ___ girl, ___

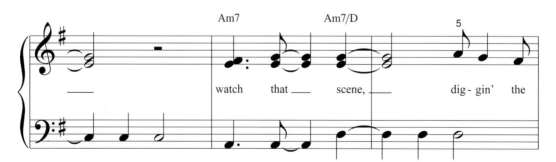

___ watch that ___ scene, ___ dig - gin' the

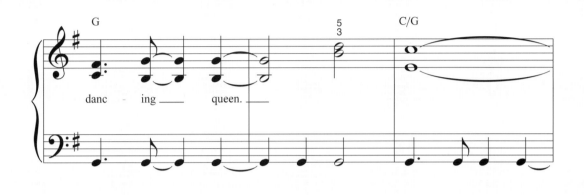

danc - ing _____ queen. _____

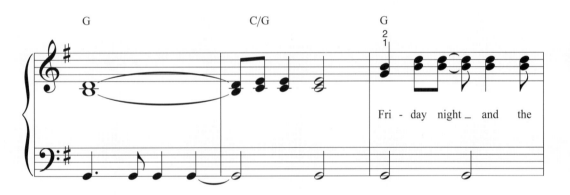

Fri - day night _ and the

lights are low, _____

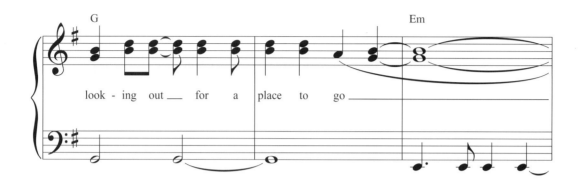

look - ing out __ for a place to go __

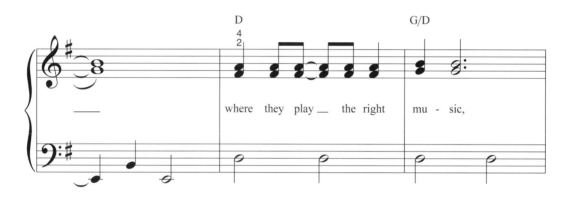

__ where they play __ the right mu - sic,

get - ting in __ the swing. __ You come to look for __ a

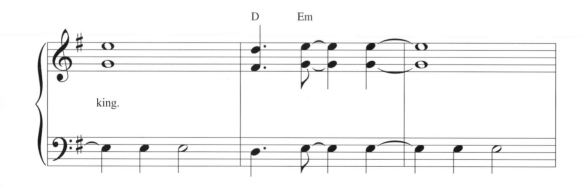

king.

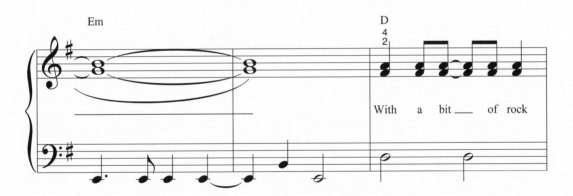

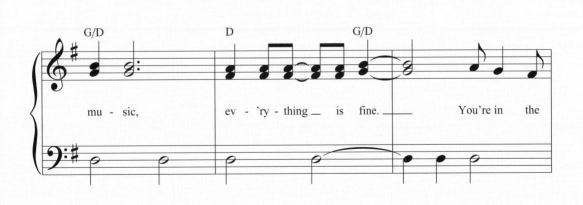

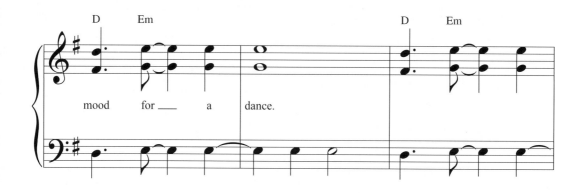

mood for ___ a dance.

And when ___ you get the ___ chance...

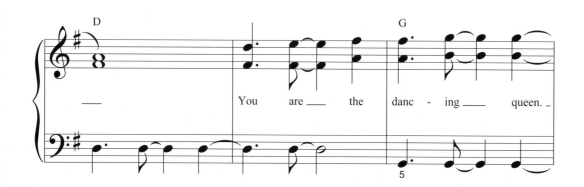

___ You are ___ the danc - ing ___ queen. ___

___ Young and ___ sweet, ___ on - ly

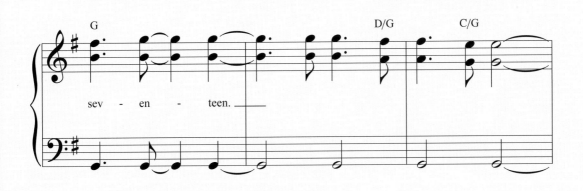

sev - en - teen.

Danc - ing ___ queen, ___

feel the ___ beat ___ from the tam - bour - ine, ___

___ oh yeah. ___

EVERY BREATH YOU TAKE

Music and Lyrics by STING

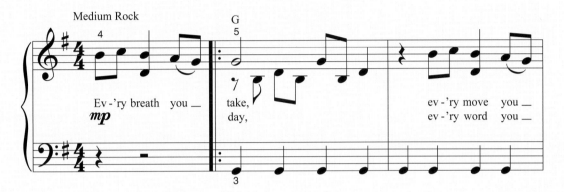

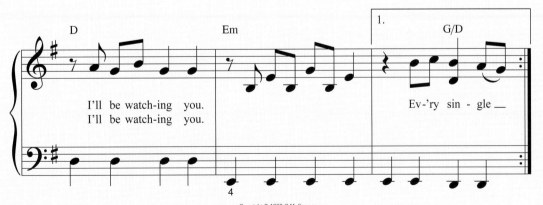

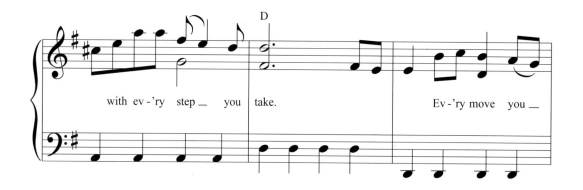

ev -'ry smile you fake, ev -'ry claim you stake, I'll be watch-ing you.

Ev -'ry move you make, ev -'ry step you take,

I'll be watch-ing you.

I'll be watch-ing you.

Material Girl

Words and Music by PETER BROWN
and ROBERT RANS

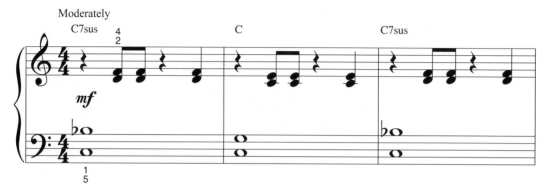

Some boys kiss __ me, some boys hug __ me
Some boys ro - mance, some boys slow __ dance.

I think they're O. K. _____ If they don't give __ me
That's all right with me. _____ If they can't raise __ my

prop - er cred - it,   I just walk a - way. _____
in - t'rest then ___ I have to let them be. _____

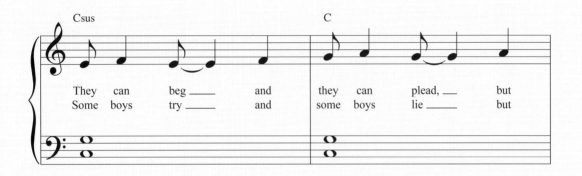

They can beg _____ and they can plead, ___ but
Some boys try _____ and some boys lie _____ but

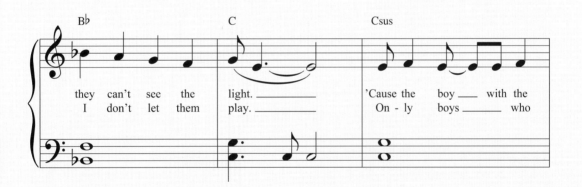

they can't see the light. _____ 'Cause the boy ___ with the
I don't let them play. _____ On - ly boys _____ who

cold hard cash ___ is al - ways Mis - ter Right. _ 'Cause we are
save their pen - nies make my rain - y day. ___ 'Cause they are

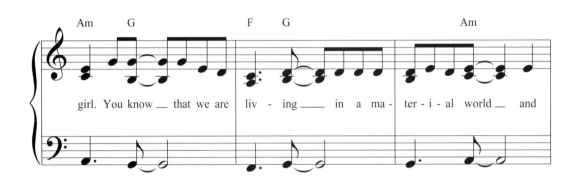

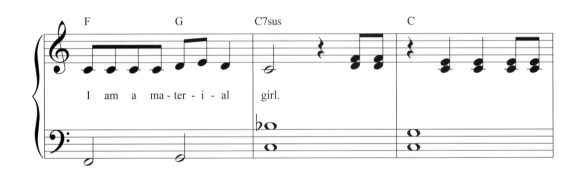

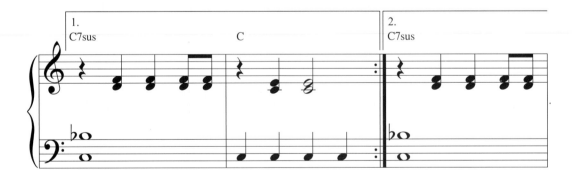

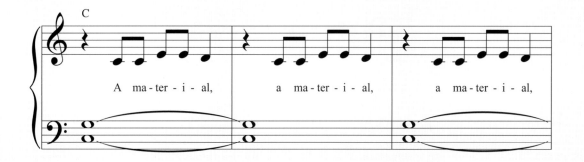

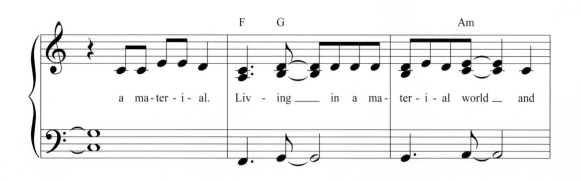

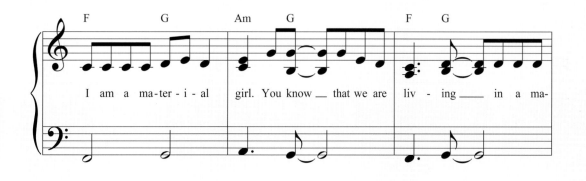

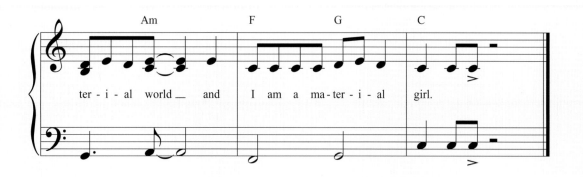

Crazy Little Thing Called Love

Words and Music by
FREDDIE MERCURY

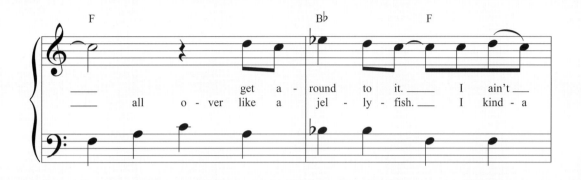

get a - round   to   it. ____   I   ain't ____
all   o - ver   like   a   jel - ly - fish. ____   I   kind - a

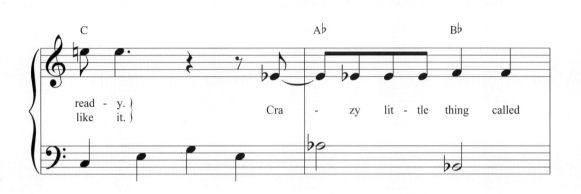

read - y.   }
like   it.   }
Cra - zy   lit - tle   thing   called

love.   Well,   this   thing __   There goes   my

ba - by; ____   she knows ____   how to rock and   roll. __

She drives __ me cra - zy. __

She gives me

hot and cold fe - ver. She leaves me in a cool, cool sweat.

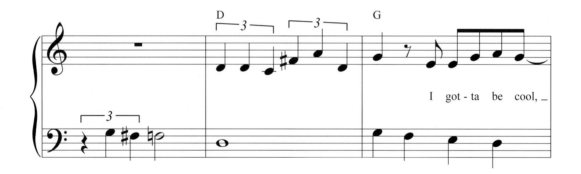

I got - ta be cool, __

re - lax, __ a - get hip, __ a - get

on my tracks. Take a back seat, hitch-hike ____ and take a

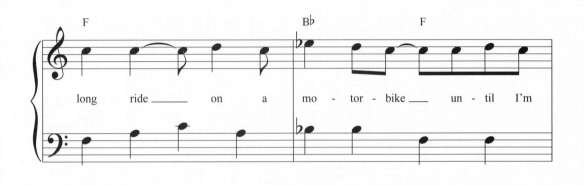

long ride ____ on a mo - tor - bike ____ un - til I'm

read - y. Cra - zy lit - tle thing called

love, hey, cra - zy lit - tle thing called love.

Billie Jean

Words and Music by
MICHAEL JACKSON

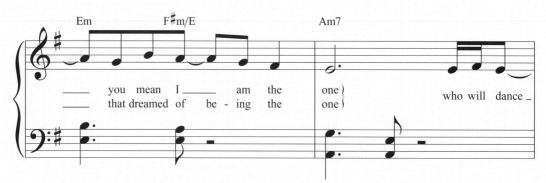

on the floor ___ in the round?

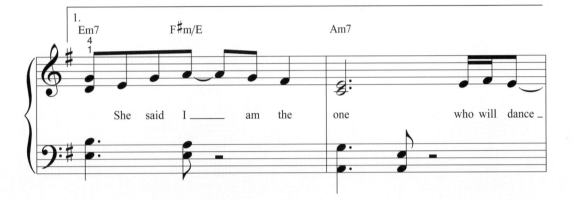

1.

She said I ___ am the one who will dance ___

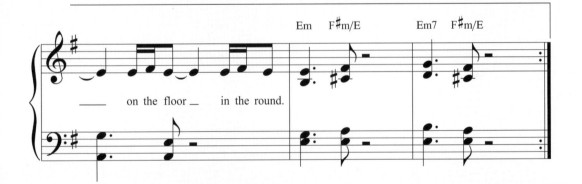

___ on the floor ___ in the round.

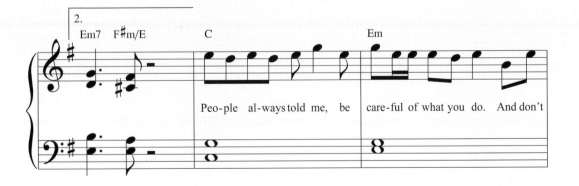

2.

Peo-ple al-ways told me, be care-ful of what you do. And don't

go a - round break - in' young girls' hearts. ___ And

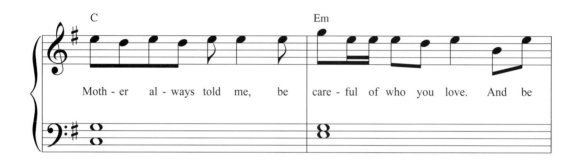

Moth - er al - ways told me, be care - ful of who you love. And be

care - ful of what you do 'cause the lie be - comes __ the truth. Hey. ___

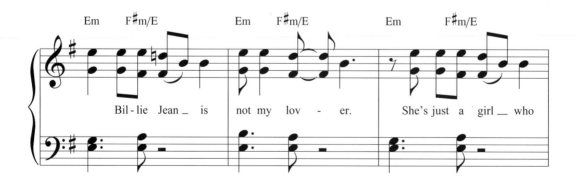

Bil - lie Jean __ is not my lov - er. She's just a girl __ who

claims that I _____ am the one, _____ but the kid ___ is not my son. ___

_____ She says I _____ am the one, _____ but the

kid ___ is not my son. ___

ONE HEADLIGHT

Words and Music by
JAKOB DYLAN

Moderately

mf So long a-go, I don't re-mem-ber when, ___ that's

when they say I lost my on-ly friend. Well, they said she died eas-y of a

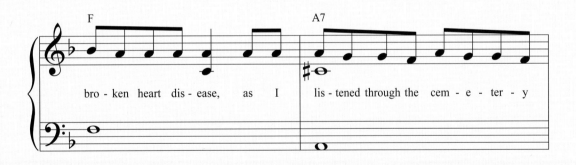

bro-ken heart dis-ease, as I lis-tened through the cem-e-ter-y

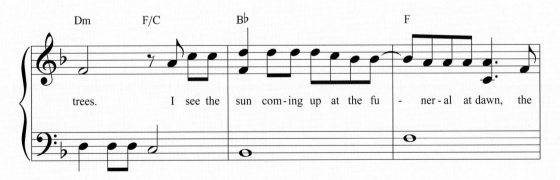

trees. I see the sun com-ing up at the fu - ner-al at dawn, the

long bro - ken arm of hu - man law. Now it

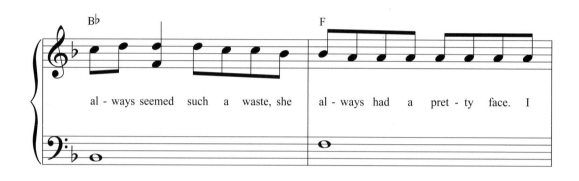

al - ways seemed such a waste, she al - ways had a pret - ty face. I

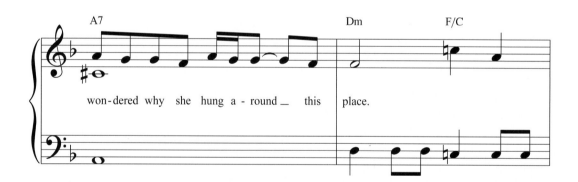

won - dered why she hung a - round __ this place.

Hey, hey, __ hey! __

Come on, try a lit-tle, noth-ing is for-ev-er.

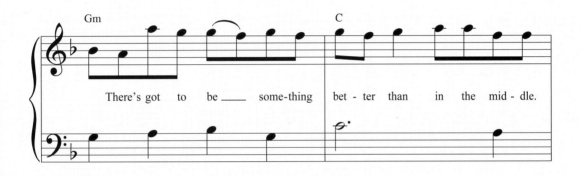

There's got to be ___ some-thing bet-ter than in the mid-dle.

But me and Cin-der-el-la, we put it all to-geth-er.

We can drive it home with one ___ head-light.

IRIS

Words and Music by
JOHN RZEZNIK

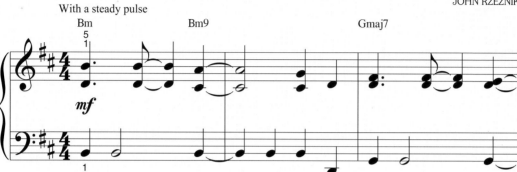

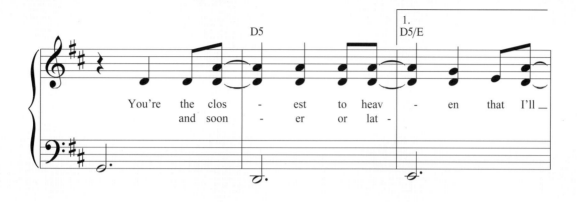

You're the clos - est to heav - en that I'll
and soon - er or lat - en

ev - er be, and I don't wan - na go

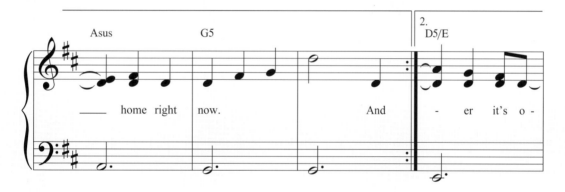

home right now. And er it's o -

- ver. I just don't wan - na miss

_____ you to - night. And I

don't want the world _____ to see me

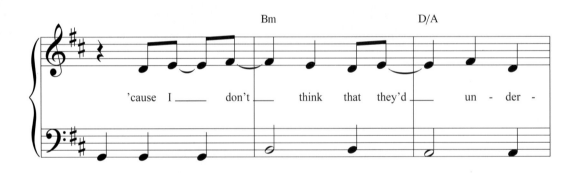

'cause I _____ don't _____ think that they'd _____ un - der -

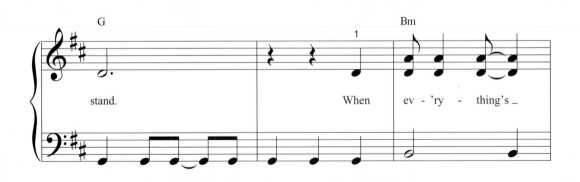

stand. When ev - 'ry - thing's _

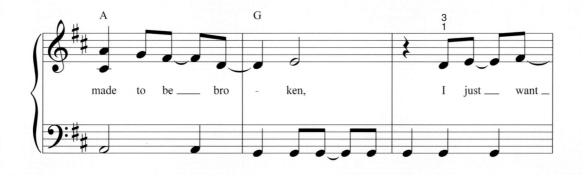

made to be ___ bro - ken,   I just ___ want ___

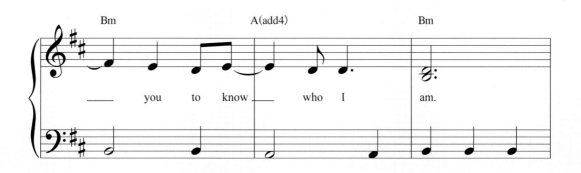

___ you to know ___ who I am.

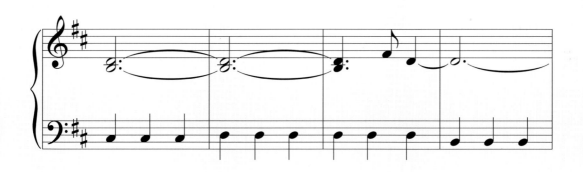

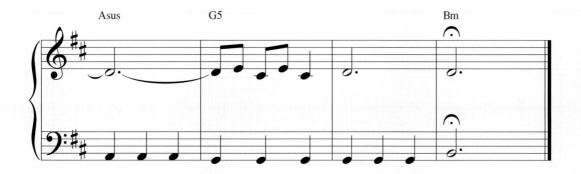

Words by ROB THOMAS
Music by ROB THOMAS and ITAAL SHUR

Medium Latin Rock

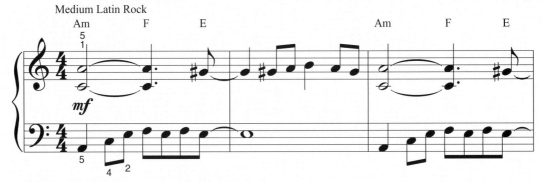

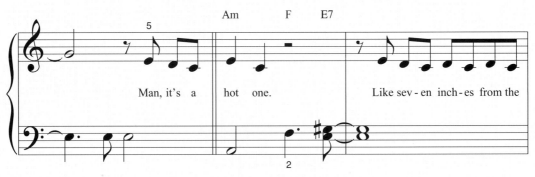

Man, it's a hot one. Like sev-en inch-es from the mid-day sun. ___ Well, I hear your whis-per and the

words melt ev-'ry one. But you stay so cool. ___

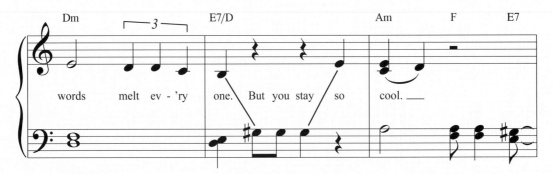

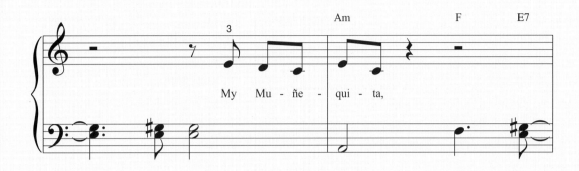

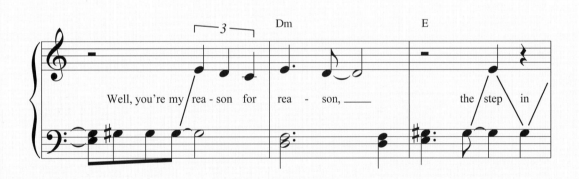

good e-nough, I would give my world to lift you up. I could change

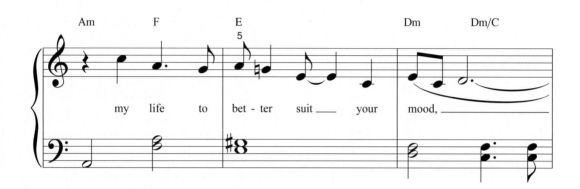

my life to bet - ter suit ___ your mood, ___

___ 'cause you're / so smooth. ___ And it's

just like the o - cean un - der the moon. Well, it's the

same as the e-mo-tion that I get from you.___ You

got the kind of lov-in' that can be so smooth._____

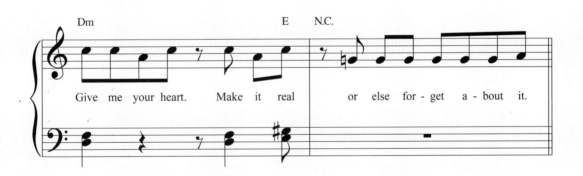

Give me your heart. Make it real or else for-get a-bout it.

Play 4 times

Let's don't for-get a-bout it.

100 Years

Words and Music by
JOHN ONDRASIK

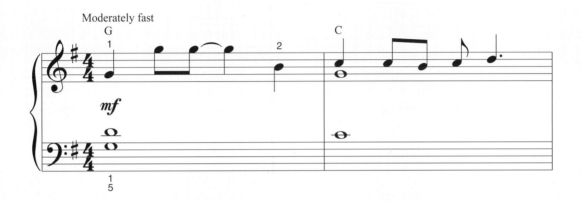

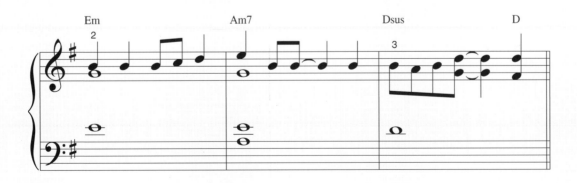

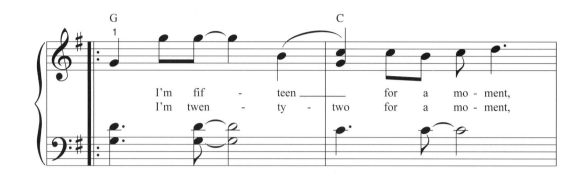

I'm fif - teen _____ for a mo - ment,
I'm twen - ty - two for a mo - ment,

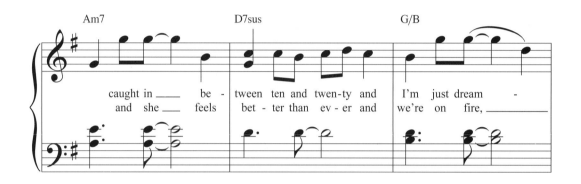

caught in _____ be - tween ten and twen-ty and I'm just dream -
and she _____ feels bet - ter than ev - er and we're on fire, _____

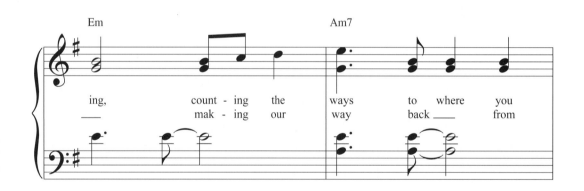

ing, count - ing the ways to where you
_____ mak - ing our way back _____ from

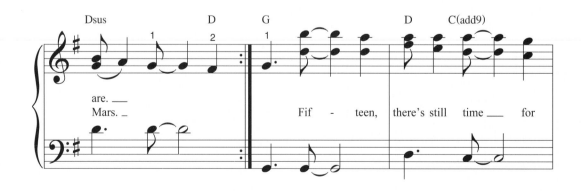

are. _____
Mars. _____ Fif - teen, there's still time _____ for

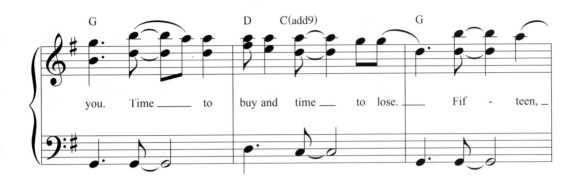

you. Time _____ to buy and time ___ to lose. ___ Fif - teen, _

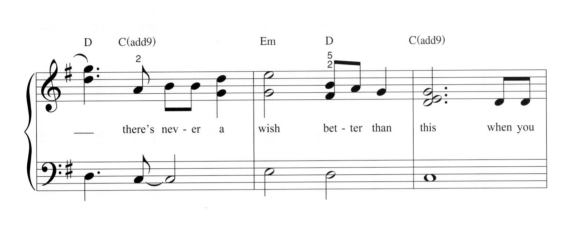

_ there's nev - er a wish bet - ter than this when you

on - ly got ___ a hun-dred years to live.

BOULEVARD OF BROKEN DREAMS

Words by BILLIE JOE
Music by GREEN DAY

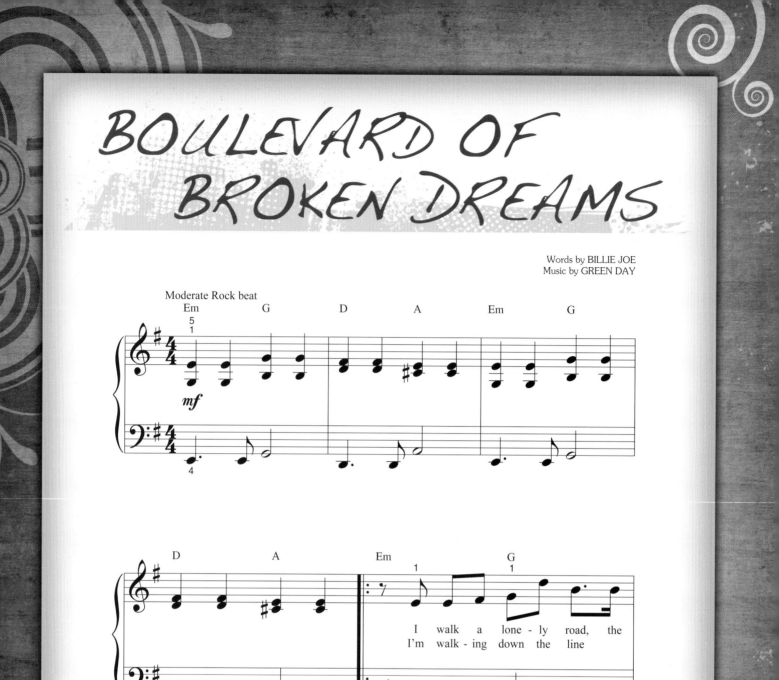

I walk a lone - ly road, the
I'm walk - ing down the line

on - ly one that I ____ have ev - er
that di - vides me some - where in my

known. I don't know where it goes,
mind. On the bor - der - line

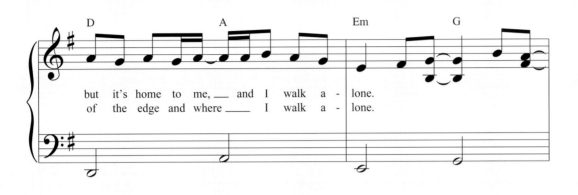

but it's home to me, __ and I walk a - lone.
of the edge and where __ I walk a - lone.

I walk this emp - ty street
Read be - tween the lines of

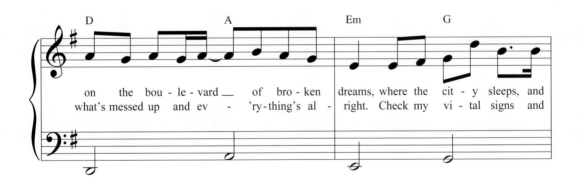

on the bou - le - vard __ of bro - ken dreams, where the cit - y sleeps, and
what's messed up and ev - 'ry - thing's al - right. Check my vi - tal signs and

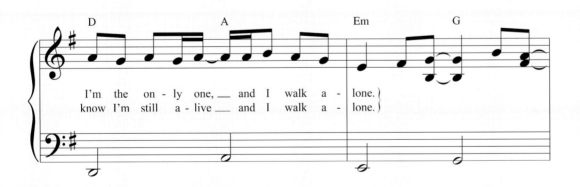

I'm the on - ly one, __ and I walk a - lone.)
know I'm still a - live __ and I walk a - lone.)

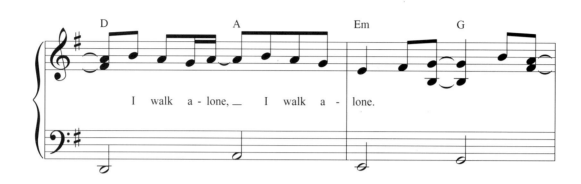

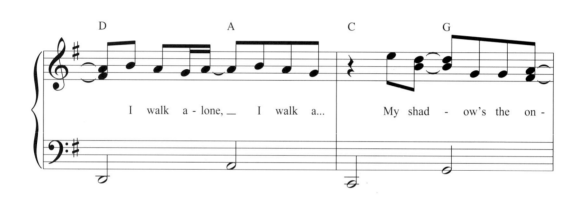

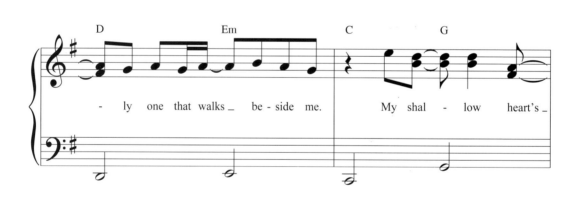

some-one out there ___ will find me. 'Til then ___ I walk ___

___ a - lone.

Ah, _____ ah, _____ ah, _____ ah.

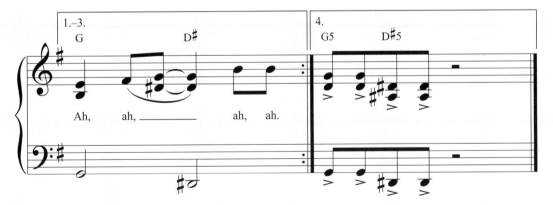

Ah, ah, _____ ah, ah.

CLOCKS

Words and Music by GUY BERRYMAN,
JON BUCKLAND, WILL CHAMPION
and CHRIS MARTIN

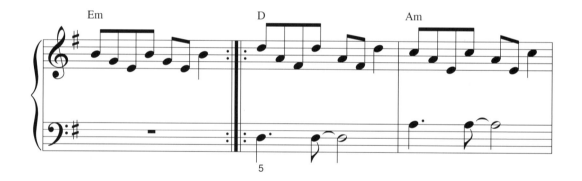

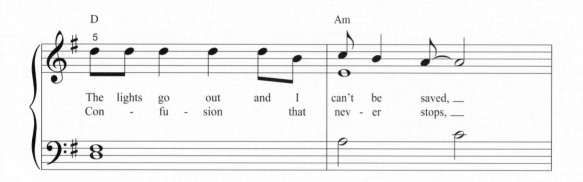

The lights go out and I can't be saved, ___
Con - fu - sion that nev - er stops, ___

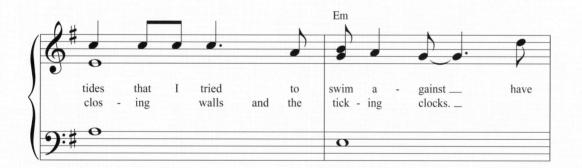

tides that I tried to swim a - gainst ___ have
clos - ing walls and the tick - ing clocks. ___

brought me down up - on my knees. ___
Gon - na come back and take you home. ___ I

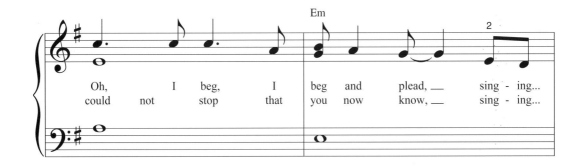

Oh,   I beg,   I   beg   and   plead, __   sing - ing...
could   not   stop   that   you   now   know, __   sing - ing...

come   out   with   things   un -   said. __   Shoot   an   ap -   ple
come   out   up -   on   my   seas, __   curse   missed   op -   por -

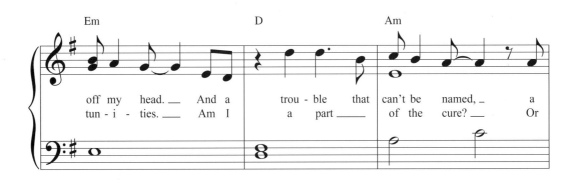

off   my   head. __   And   a   trou -   ble   that   can't   be   named, __   a
tun - i - ties. __   Am   I   a   part ___   of   the   cure? __   Or

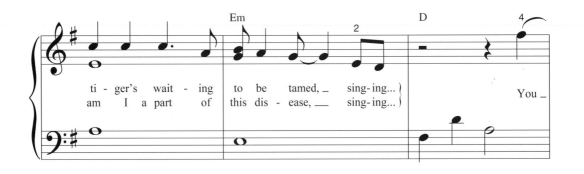

ti - ger's   wait -   ing   to   be   tamed, _   sing - ing...)
am   I   a   part   of   this   dis - ease, __   sing - ing...)   You _

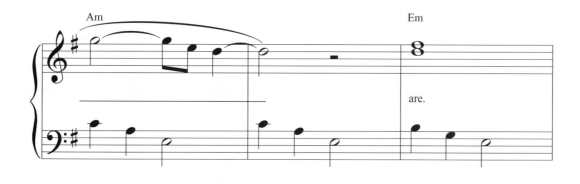

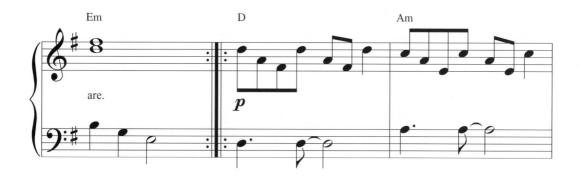

Repeat and Fade | **Optional Ending**

HAPPY

Words and Music by
PHARRELL WILLIAMS

Moderately fast

It might seem cra - zy what I'm 'bout to say.

Sun - shine, __ she's

here; you can take a break. I'm a

hot air bal - loon __ that could go to space

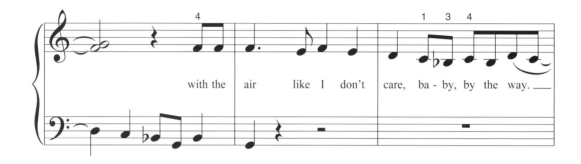

with the   air   like I don't   care, ba - by, by the way. ___

Huh! ___   Be-cause I'm   hap - py. ___
Clap a - long

if   you   feel ___   like   a   room   with - out   a   roof.

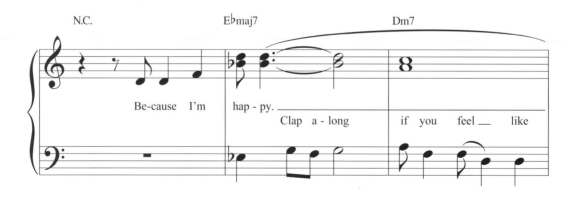

Be-cause I'm   hap - py. ___   if   you   feel ___ like
Clap a - long

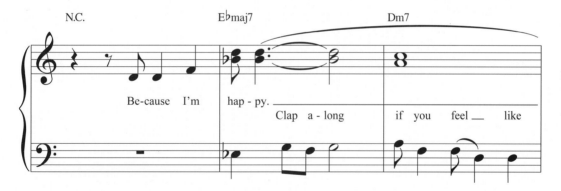

RADIOACTIVE

Words and Music by DANIEL REYNOLDS,
BENJAMIN McKEE, DANIEL SERMON,
ALEXANDER GRANT and JOSH MOSSER

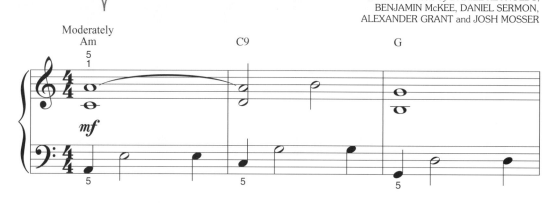

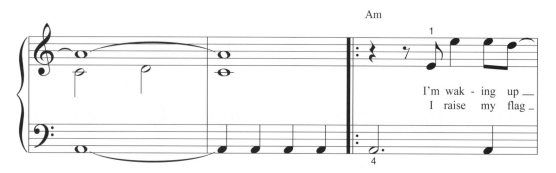

I'm wak - ing up
I raise my flag

to ash and dust;
and dye my clothes.

I wipe my
It's a rev - o -

brow and I sweat my
lu - tion, I sup -

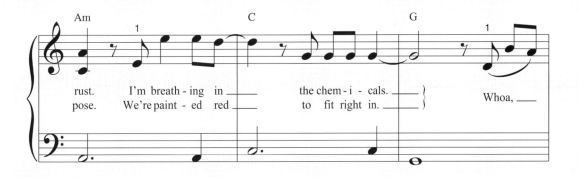

rust. I'm breath - ing in ____ the chem - i - cals. ____
pose. We're paint - ed red ____ to fit right in. ____ Whoa, ____

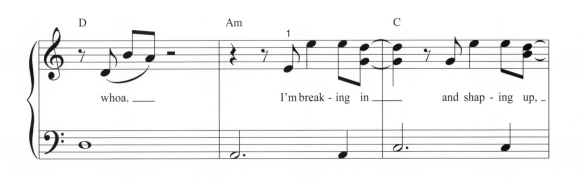

whoa. ____ I'm break - ing in ____ and shap - ing up, ____

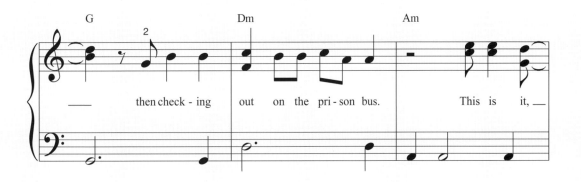

then check - ing out on the pri - son bus. This is it, ____

____ the A - poc - a - lypse. ____ Whoa. ____ I'm wak - ing

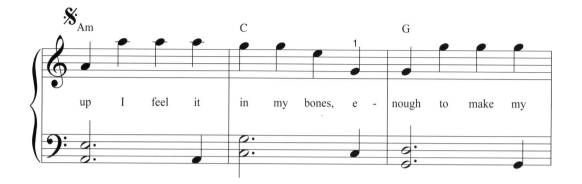

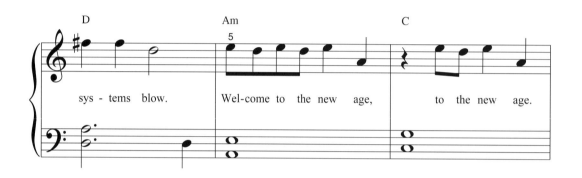

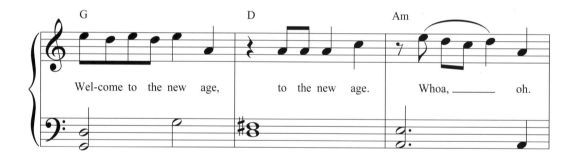

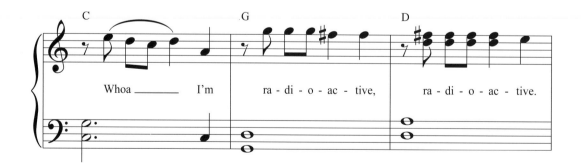

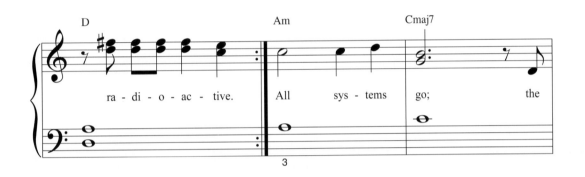

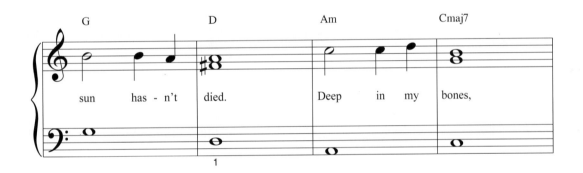

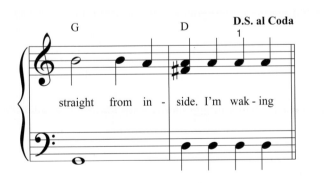

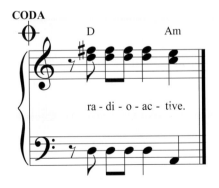

SOME NIGHTS

Words and Music by JEFF BHASKER,
ANDREW DOST, JACK ANTONOFF
and NATE RUESS

Moderate March

Some nights I stay _ up cash-in' in my bad luck, _ some nights I call it a _

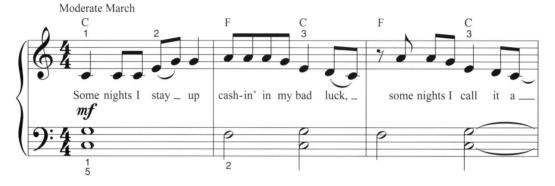

_ draw. Some nights I wish _ that my lips could build a cas - tle, _

some nights I wish they'd just fall _ off. But I still wake up, _ I still

see your ghost. _ Oh Lord, I'm still not sure _ what I stand for, oh. Whoa, _

_____ what do I stand for? _____ What do I stand for? Most nights, I don't

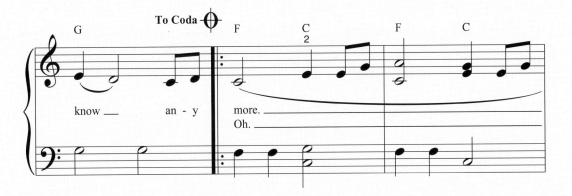

To Coda

know _____ an - y more. _____
Oh. _____

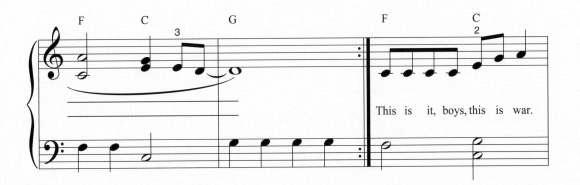

This is it, boys, this is war.

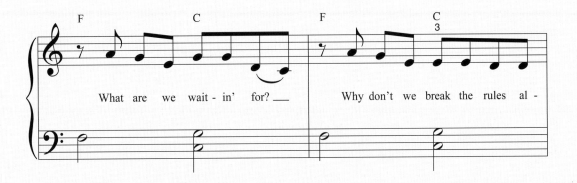

What are we wait - in' for? _____ Why don't we break the rules al -

read - y? I was nev - er one ___ to be-lieve the hype, ___

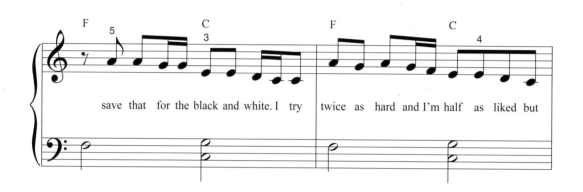

save that for the black and white. I try twice as hard and I'm half as liked but

here they come a - gain to jack my style. That's al -

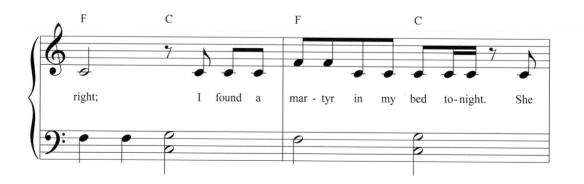

right; I found a mar - tyr in my bed to-night. She

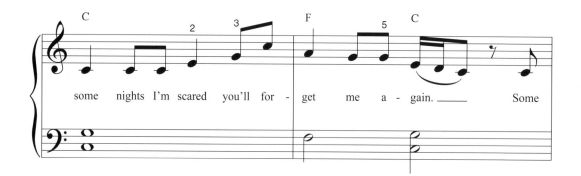

some nights I'm scared you'll for - get me a - gain. _____ Some

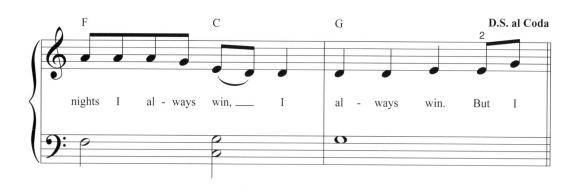

nights I al - ways win, ___ I al - ways win. But I

D.S. al Coda

CODA

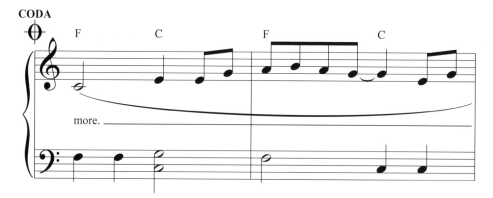

more. _____

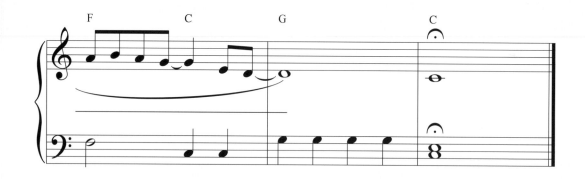